Gone Forever!
Diplodocus

Rupert Matthews

Heinemann
LIBRARY

www.heinemann.co.uk/library
Visit our website to find out more information about Heinemann Library books.

To order:

 Phone ++44 (0)1865 888066
Send a fax to ++44 (0)1865 314091
Visit the Heinemann Bookshop at www.heinemann.co.uk/library to browse our catalogue and
order online.

First published in Great Britain by Heinemann Library, Halley Court, Jordan Hill, Oxford OX2 8EJ, a part of Harcourt Education. Heinemann is a registered trademark of Harcourt Education Ltd.

© Harcourt Education Ltd 2003.
First published in paperback in 2004.
The moral right of the proprietor has been asserted.

Editorial: Andrew Farrow and Dan Nunn
Design: Ron Kamen and Paul Davies & Associates
Illustrations: Maureen and Gordon Gray, James Field (SGA) and Darren Lingard
Picture Research: Maria Joannou, Rebecca Sodergren and Frances Topp
Production: Viv Hichens
Originated by Ambassador Litho Ltd
Printed and bound in China by South China Printing Company

07 06 05 04 03   08 07 06 05 04
10 9 8 7 6 5 4 3 2 1   10 9 8 7 6 5 4 3 2 1
ISBN 0 431 16604 8   ISBN 0 431 16611 0
(hardback)   (paperback)

British Library Cataloguing in Publication Data
Matthews, Rupert
Diplodocus. - (Gone forever)
1. Diplodocus - Juvenile literature
I. Title
567.9'13

Acknowledgements
The Publishers are grateful to the following for permission to reproduce photographs: Ardea pp. 4, 6 (Francois Gohier), 10 (Francois Gohier), 18 (Francois Gohier), 20 (Francois Gohier), 24 (Francois Gohier); FLPA/Mark Newman p. 14; Natural History Museum, London pp. 12, 22, 26; REUTERS/Rodolfo Coria p. 16; Science Photo Library p. 8.

Cover photo reproduced with permission of Ardea/Francois Gohier.

Our thanks to Dr David Norman and Dr Angela Milner for their assistance in the preparation of this book.

Every effort has been made to contact copyright holders of any material reproduced in this book. Any omissions will be rectified in subsequent printings if notice is given to the Publishers.

Contents

Some words are shown in bold, **like this**.
You can find out what they mean by looking in the Glossary.

Gone forever!

Millions of years ago there were many different types of animals. Most of these animals have now completely vanished. They are said to be **extinct**. Scientists study extinct animals by digging their **fossils** out of very old rocks.

One of these extinct animals was called Diplodocus. This massive creature lived in North America about 150 million years ago. Most of the other animals and plants which lived at that time are also now extinct.

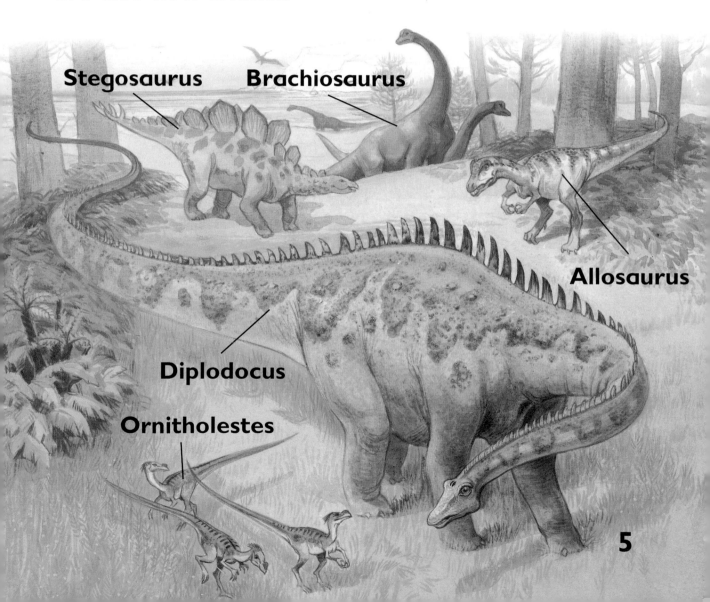

Stegosaurus

Brachiosaurus

Allosaurus

Diplodocus

Ornitholestes

Where Diplodocus lived

Scientists called **geologists** study rocks. They use the rocks to find out what an area was like when the rocks were formed. They can even tell what the weather was like!

Diplodocus lived in areas where it rained heavily for some of the year. At other times it was dry. The land was flat with wide rivers, lakes and swamps. There were some open spaces, but also many trees and other plants.

Plants

Sometimes plants are turned into **fossils**. These fossils tell us what plants were growing nearby when the rocks were formed. Animals are not the only things that can become **extinct**. Plants can become extinct, too.

fossils of ginkgo leaves

There were no grasses or flowers when Diplodocus was alive. Instead **ferns**, **fir trees** and **cycads** were common. There were also many plants that are now extinct.

9

Living with Diplodocus

Fossils show that many other animals lived at the same time as Diplodocus. Some of these creatures were also large **dinosaurs**. This picture shows some **Stegosaurus** fossils. Smaller animals have also been found, such as **mammals**, frogs and small **reptiles**.

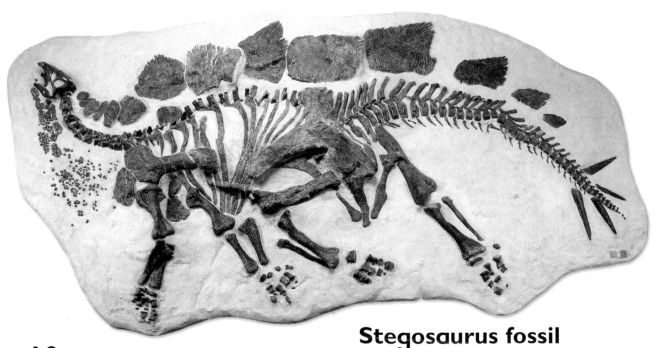

Stegosaurus fossil

Stegosaurus

Ornitholestes

Stegosaurus was a plant-eating dinosaur. It grew to be about 9 metres long and weighed about 2 tonnes. The spikes on its tail were used to fight off attackers. Smaller dinosaurs included **Ornitholestes**. Ornitholestes hunted lizards and other small animals.

What was Diplodocus?

Several **fossils** of Diplodocus have been found. The bones have been dug out of the ground and fitted together. The bones show what Diplodocus looked like.

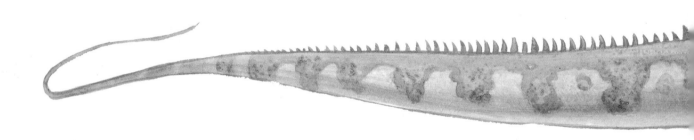

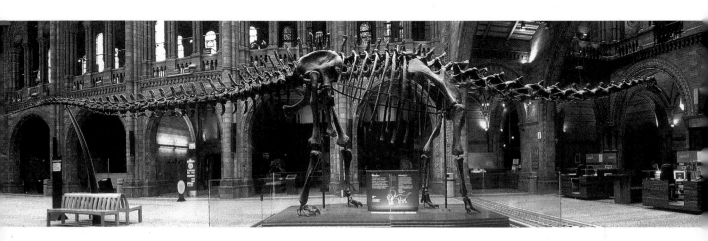

Diplodocus had a very long neck and an even longer tail. It was about 27 metres long and walked on four very strong legs. Diplodocus ate only plants. It **digested** these in its massive stomach.

Diplodocus eggs

dinosaur egg fossils

Scientists have found **fossils** of eggs laid by **dinosaurs** similar to Diplodocus. The eggs are about the size of footballs.

Scientists have not found any Diplodocus nests, so
we do not know what they look like. But perhaps
the mother Diplodocus dug a shallow pit in soft
ground with her feet. Eggs would probably have
been left in the nest until they were ready to **hatch**.

Growing up

Fossils of baby **dinosaurs** show that they were very small compared to adults. They grew quickly. A baby Diplodocus probably doubled in weight every month.

fossil of the head of a baby dinosaur like Diplodocus

Diplodocus babies probably lived in dense forests. There they could hide among the leaves and plants. They would be safe from attack by large hunting dinosaurs. They probably stayed in the forests for about five years while they grew bigger and bigger.

A herd on the move

Fossils of footprints made by dinosaurs like Diplodocus have been found in rocks. These footprints show that Diplodocus lived in small **herds**. Only footprints of adult or half-grown animals have been found in herds.

18

Some scientists think that the half-grown animals stayed in the centre of each herd. The larger animals could then protect them. Other scientists think the younger animals followed the adults.

Reaching for food

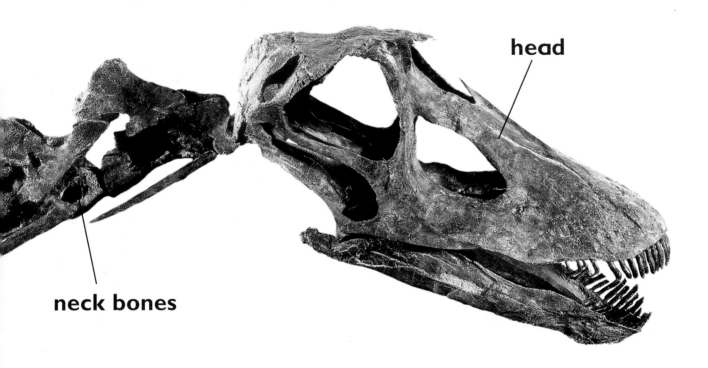

head

neck bones

Diplodocus had a very long neck. **Fossil** bones show that the neck and head were usually held straight out in front of the body. The long tail helped to balance the heavy neck.

Diplodocus could bend its neck from side to side or up and down. It could reach many different plants while standing still. Diplodocus ate all the plants it could reach, and then moved on.

Unusual teeth

The head of Diplodocus was small compared to its body. Its jaw muscles were quite weak. Its teeth were long and straight like the teeth of a comb. This meant Diplodocus could not chew its food.

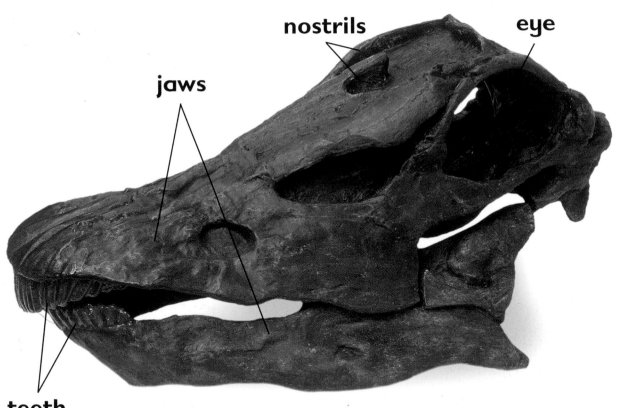

nostrils

eye

jaws

teeth

Scientists have worked out that Diplodocus had a special way of eating. It closed its mouth around a tree branch, and then pulled backwards. The teeth dragged the leaves off the tree like a garden rake, leaving the branches behind. Then Diplodocus swallowed the leaves whole.

Danger!

Scientists have found **fossils** of two-legged **dinosaurs** with long sharp teeth. These were dinosaurs that killed and ate other dinosaurs. This is an **Allosaurus** skeleton. Allosaurus lived at the same time as Diplodocus.

Allosaurus was up to 15 metres long and was
very strong. It used its claws and teeth to attack
other dinosaurs. Allosaurus probably attacked
small, young Diplodocus. These would be easier
to kill than the larger adults.

Fighting Diplodocus

Diplodocus had a long tail with strong muscles. It could swish its tail from side to side very quickly. Diplodocus could use the end of its tail like a powerful whip.

Scientists think that maybe Diplodocus used its tail to defend itself. **Allosaurus** would attack using its teeth and claws. If Diplodocus hit Allosaurus with its tail, the attacker could be badly hurt. Diplodocus could then escape.

Where did Diplodocus live?

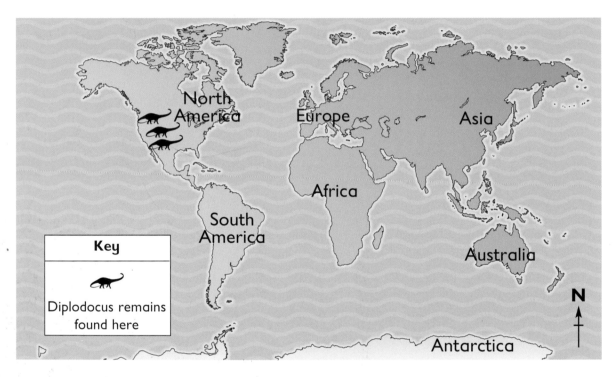

Key

Diplodocus remains found here

North America

Europe

Asia

Africa

South America

Australia

Antarctica

N

Diplodocus **fossils** have been found in North America. These show that Diplodocus lived in the western part of that continent. Other **dinosaurs** that looked similar to Diplodocus have been found in Asia, Europe and parts of Africa.

When did Diplodocus live?

Diplodocus lived between 155 and 144 million years ago (mya). This was during the period that scientists call the Jurassic Period. The Jurassic Period was the middle period of the Mesozoic Era, also known as the Age of the Dinosaurs.

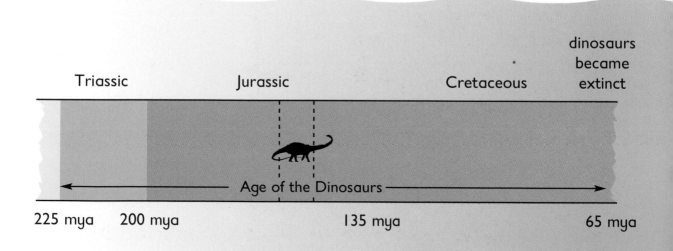

Fact file

Diplodocus fact file	
Length:	up to 27 metres
Height:	up to 6 metres
Weight:	20 tonnes
When it lived:	Late Jurassic Period, about 150 million years ago
Where it lived:	North America

How to say it

Allosaurus – al-oh-saw-rus
cycad – sigh-kadd
dinosaur – dine-oh-saw

Diplodocus – dipp-plodd-oh-kus
Stegosaurus – stegg-oh-saw-rus

Glossary

Allosaurus large meat-eating dinosaur. Allosaurus hunted Diplodocus, Stegosaurus and other plant-eating dinosaurs.

cycad type of plant that looks like a short palm tree

digest to break down food in your stomach so that it can be used by the body

dinosaur one of a large group of extinct reptiles that lived on land. Dinosaurs lived on Earth between 225 and 65 million years ago.

extinct an animal or plant is extinct when there are none of its kind left alive

ferns plants with long, curly leaves that grow from the ground

fir trees trees that keep their tough, waxy leaves all year round. Christmas trees are a type of fir tree.

fossil remains of a plant or animal, usually found in rocks. Sometimes the remains have been turned into rock. Most fossils are bones or teeth because these hard parts are more easily preserved. Some fossils are traces of animals, such as their footprints.

geologist scientist who studies rocks

hatch to break out of an egg

herd group of animals living together and helping each other

mammal animal with hair or fur. Mammals give birth to live young instead of laying eggs.

Ornitholestes type of dinosaur that lived at the same time as Diplodocus. It ate lizards and other small animals.

reptile cold-blooded animals such as a modern snake or lizard

Stegosaurus type of plant-eating dinosaur that lived at the same time as Diplodocus

Find out more

These are some books about dinosaurs:
Big Book of Dinosaurs, Angela Wilkes (Dorling Kindersley, 2001)
Dinosaur Park, Nick Denchfield (Macmillan, 1998)
Diplodocus, Michael P. Goecke (Abdo Publishing Company, 2002)

Look on these websites for more information:
www.enchantedlearning.com/subjects/dinos
www.oink.demon.co.uk/topics/dinosaur.htm
www.carnegiemuseums.org/cmnh/exhibits/dippy

Index